How to be a...
BMX CHAMPION

James Nixon

W
FRANKLIN WATTS
LONDON • SYDNEY

First published in 2015 by
Franklin Watts
338 Euston Road
London NW1 3BH

Franklin Watts Australia
Level 17/207 Kent Street
Sydney NSW 2000

© 2015 Franklin Watts

ISBN 978 1 4451 3617 2
Library eBook ISBN 978 1 4451 3619 6

Dewey classification number: 796.6

In preparation of this book, all due care has been exercised with regard to the advice, activities and techniques depicted. The publishers regret that they can accept no liability for any loss or injury sustained. When learning a new activity, it is important to get expert tuition and to follow a manufacturer's instructions.

A CIP catalogue record for this publication is available from the British Library.

Planning and production by Discovery Books Limited
Managing Editor: Paul Humphrey
Editor: James Nixon
Design: sprout.uk.com
Picture research: James Nixon

Printed in China

Franklin Watts is a division of Hachette Children's Books, an Hachette UK Company.
www.hachette.co.uk

Photo acknowledgements: Cover image (Alamy: Josh Chapel/Southcreek Global/ZUMA Press) Alamy: pp. 9 top (Chris Hunt/Southcreek Global/ZUMA Press), 9 bottom (Rainer Jensen/EPA), 11 bottom (Robert Ghement/EPA), 12 (Charlie Newman/U-T San Diego/ZUMA Press), 14 (Simon Balson), 15 top and bottom (Allstar Picture Library), 17 bottom (Simon Balson), 18 (Troy Wayryen/NewSport/ ZUMA Press), 19 (Allstar Picture Library), 21 top (Keith Morris), 22 (DPA Picture Alliance), 23 top (Chris Hunt/Southcreek Global/ZUMA Press), 25 bottom (Chris Rabior), 28 (Josh Chapel/Southcreek Global/ZUMA Press), 29 top (Joe Scarnici/ZUMA Press). Mongoose Bicycles: p. 7. Shutterstock: pp. 4 (homydesign), 5 top (Haslam Photography), 5 bottom (homydesign), 6 (homydesign), 8 (Tim Large), 10 (homydesign), 11 top (homydesign), 13 top and bottom (homydesign), 16 (homydesign), 17 top (homydesign), 20 (de2marco), 21 middle (Haslam Photography), 21 bottom (homydesign), 23 bottom (homydesign), 24 (homydesign), 25 top (homydesign), 26 (homydesign), 27 top (Michelle Marsan), 27 bottom (Rihardzz), 29 middle and bottom (Haslam Photography).

Every attempt has been made to clear copyright. Should there be any inadvertent omission please apply to the publisher for rectification.

CONTENTS

All words in **bold** can be found in the glossary on page 31

BMX RACING AND FREESTYLE

BMX is an extreme cycling sport for daring athletes. There are two main types of competition in BMX. In BMX racing, riders race each other on tracks. The tracks contain sharp turns, hills and bumps. The other type of BMX riding is called freestyle. Freestyle riders perform tricks on their bikes in front of judges.

A LITTLE BIT OF HISTORY

BMX riding began in the late 1960s in California, USA, when teenagers started racing their bicycles on self-built dirt tracks. It was around the same time that motocross (dirt racing on motorbikes) became popular. BMX stands for 'bicycle motocross'. By the 1980s BMX competitions were being held across the world. Today the sport is more popular than ever.

AN OLYMPIC SPORT

In 2008, BMX racing became part of the Summer Olympics. At the start of a race, up to eight riders launch themselves down a high ramp on to the course. A race is just one lap of the track and lasts for less than a minute. Riders can fly over the jumps using any part of the track. The battle for first place is fierce. The riders can touch each other as long as they don't cause a crash.

BMX racing is a fast and dramatic sport.

RECORD BREAKERS

In 2013 BMX legend Kevin Robinson from the USA broke the world record for the highest jump off a **vert** ramp. He soared higher than a house, over eight metres into the air.

Kevin Robinson jumps high and no-handed in a vert competition.

FREESTYLING

Freestyle BMX riders love the thrill of pulling off amazing tricks and stunts. There are many types of competition for freestyle riders. In some events riders perform tricks on obstacles in a skate park or on rails, steps and platforms you might find in the street.

Other riders show off their tricks on flat ground or on massive dirt jumps. In vert competitions, freestylers take turns on a huge **halfpipe** ramp to do crazy stunts in mid-air. The judges award points to a freestyler for their tricks and decide on the winner.

BMX riders can do amazing tricks in skate parks.

KNOW YOUR BIKE

The first step to riding BMX is to get a bike! BMX bikes are built in a different way to road bikes. They are small, extremely strong and can be steered easily. They also weigh a lot less than road bikes. This design makes it easier to do jumps and tricks.

In BMX racing, the lighter the bike the better, but it also has to be strong enough for jumping and landing.

CHOOSING A BIKE

The bike you need depends on the type of riding you want it for. BMX racers need bikes that are fast and lightweight with tyres that will grip the track surface. Freestyle bikes have a sturdy frame and extra parts added on for stunt riding, such as **pegs** that the rider can place their feet on. The handlebars and seat can also be spun completely around.

It is not wise to buy a really expensive bike if you are a beginner because you are likely to break parts when you are learning. Be aware, though, that really cheap bikes will fall apart more easily.

AT THE BIKE SHOP

Don't just choose the BMX bike that looks the best. You need to find a bike that works for you. A good bike shop will help you find the right BMX bike. They will check that the bike fits your size. Make sure you test ride the bike to ensure that it feels comfortable and easy to handle.

Handlebars – can be spun around without tangling the brake cable inside

Brakes – Freestyle bikes come with front and rear brakes. Race bikes usually have rear brakes only.

Saddle – is often set up low as racers rarely sit down

Axle pegs – Freestyle riders ride on these tubes attached to the wheel to do tricks.

Frame – can be covered in padding to protect the rider in a crash

Fork

Pedals

Cranks – These arms attached to the pedals take a lot of bumps and must be strong.

Chain – transmits power to the wheels

Tyres – have to be knobbly for dirt surfaces. Freestyle riders who do tricks in skate parks and paved areas use smoother tyres.

GEAR GUIDE

Staying safe is an important part of being a BMX rider. Riders can fall or crash at any time, especially when they are learning. Make sure you have the right equipment to protect your body.

HELMETS

A helmet is the most vital piece of kit. An injury to the head can be fatal. Riding without a helmet isn't worth the risk. Buy a helmet that feels comfortable to wear. It shouldn't wobble when you move, but it shouldn't squeeze your skull either. Some helmets have a **visor** that shields the eyes from dirt and the sun. Riders should also wear mouthguards that are sometimes built into the helmets.

PADDING

Many parts of the body need protection. Knees and elbows often get bumped and scraped so make sure you have some knee and elbow pads. If you are trying out tricks it is a good idea to wear pads that cover the shins too. BMX racers wear padded clothes called leathers to protect as much of their skin as possible. Gloves help you to grip the bars as well as providing protection.

BMX racers wear padded clothes for protection.

Freestylers wear knee and elbow pads when they perform tricks.

SAFETY TIPS

Be careful when you are riding in full safety gear because padding can catch on the bike and throw you off. Also, don't wear any flappy clothing that could get stuck in the bike. It is a good idea to practise tricks and skills only when other people are around in case you get injured. And never race or try tricks in the street close to traffic.

Good BMX riders even know how to fall safely! If you are falling try to stop yourself putting your hands out as this can break bones. Keep your hands tucked in and try to roll your body to soften the impact.

TOP DOG

Corey Martinez from the USA is one of the legends in freestyle BMX. Martinez concentrates his skills on street obstacles. His amazing creativity and style landed him **sponsors**, video appearances and features on the front covers of magazines. But he says what he enjoys most is… 'hanging out with friends and having a good session. Being motivated by each other and enjoying that time is the best thing!'

Cyclists tangle and crash in the Men's BMX at the 2012 London Olympics.

RACING SKILLS

Winning a BMX race takes more than strong legs. It is a test of skill and technique. The main thing that makes a rider smoother and faster on the BMX track is practice, practice, practice.

BE PREPARED

Take it slow on your first few laps of a BMX track. This will give you time to learn the track and the obstacles that are coming up. Most of the time riders are faster on the ground than they are in the air so try to stay as low as possible over the jumps. The fastest beginners are usually those who try to take the course smoothly rather than quickly.

PEDAL HARD

A BMX race is a short sprint so you need to be pedalling as hard as you can, as often as you can. While pedalling, keep your body up and out of the saddle. Your back and neck should be straight with your elbows slightly bent and your wrists rolled forward over the bars. Don't stamp down on the pedals – pedal in smooth circles.

As a race lasts about 40 seconds, your best chance of winning the race is by taking the lead into the first corner. To do that you need to learn how to get out of the **starting gate** first and accelerate fast.

BMX racers pedal fast and smooth to drive them forwards on the short course.

THE STARTING GATE

For the best start, learn how to balance at the gate with both feet already on the pedals (right). You can practise the two-footed start anywhere. Just roll up to a wall until the front wheel is touching. Put a tiny bit of pressure on your pedal to keep the wheel solid against the gate. Stand upright, relaxed and use both of your arms to balance the bike.

In a race you need to keep your eyes on the top of the gate. As soon as it drops, snap out fast by thrusting your hips into the handlebars and driving down the pedal.

With both feet on the pedals use your arms to balance the bike against the starting gate.

BRAKING

BMX racing bikes are simple. They have only one gear and just a rear brake. If you need to brake in a race, pull the lever with one or two fingers gradually and move your weight towards the back of the bike. If you are leaning forward or to the side, it will cause the bike to slide.

TOP DOG

Colombian Mariana Pajon has earned the nickname 'Queen of BMX'. Pajon started racing BMX at the age of 4 and became a world champion by the age of 9! She has since won twelve world championship titles and was the gold medal winner at the 2012 London Olympics.

HAZARDS

After racers launch out of the starting gate they rush down the starting ramp. On some tracks the ramp is big – some are scarily big. All give you the speed to get going in a hurry. During a race there are a variety of obstacles. Good riders practise tackling each obstacle one at a time until they can do it perfectly. Then, in a race, they piece it all together.

BERM TURNS

BMX courses have huge banked corners called **berms**. As you approach a berm, keep your eyes ahead and focus on the line you want to take. Learn which line is fastest. It is usually best to stay high on the outside of the berm. Good riders can hit the berms at high speed without slowing down.

Riders race around a huge berm on the Chula Vista track in California, USA.

RECORD BREAKERS

French rider Joss Daudet took the BMX world by storm in 2011. He blew away the competition on the European Tour by winning an incredible and historic 12 wins out of 12. To top it off he won the World Championships later that year, too.

JUMPING

Clever riders try not to fly too high on the jumps. They lose too much time when they do. Keeping the bike as low as possible over jumps is called 'speed-jumping'.

To jump, you need to bring the front wheel up as you hit the top of the ramp. Do this by pushing the pedal forwards and shifting your bodyweight back behind the bike. The aim is then to shift your weight so that you land perfectly and smoothly on two wheels. By landing on the **downslope** of a ramp you can build up lots of speed.

Learning to jump takes a lot of nerve and practice.

A 'double' is the classic BMX jump. Two hills are spaced apart by a gap that needs to be jumped. A 'table top' is a hill with a flat top that needs to be cleared.

...AND PUMPING

Smaller hills are called rollers. They can come at you at two, three, four at a time or more. The technique to ride these is called pumping. As your front wheel rolls over the top of the hill pump (push) the handlebars down the slope. Continue to pedal as hard as you can but keep it smooth. Pumping hills and jumps is a key skill and will increase your speed.

A group of rollers is called a rhythm section. These are all about staying loose on the bike and taking the bumps with a smooth, flowing style. The best way to learn is to watch videos of the pros in action.

A rider pumps his bike through a section of rollers.

ON TRACK

No two BMX racetracks are the same. Apart from having a starting gate and a finish line, everything else in between is different. A BMX course is carefully built and designed to provide a unique and exciting challenge to the riders.

BMX tracks can be indoors or outdoors. Some tracks are smoother than others. They can be made of tarmac or compacted mud and sand. The layout and type of obstacles varies greatly. Some tracks have lots of big jumps and fast downhill sections while others are fairly flat. A course can be just 250 metres long or over 400 metres. The width of a track can be over eight metres wide to less than three metres in places.

STARTING OUT

There are BMX tracks all over the country so it should be easy to find one near you. Most clubs and tracks offer coaching sessions to riders of all ages and abilities. You can also hire a bike and gear, to try out the sport and see if it is for you.

WORLD CHAMPIONSHIPS

The pros compete at five tracks across the world as they battle for the World Cup series. The World Championships is a separate one-off event held every year. The National BMX Centre in Manchester, UK, is the largest indoor BMX track in Europe. Since 2013 it has held rounds of the World Cup. Fans pack the stands, making it one of the most spectacular venues.

Riders fly over a table-top jump at the BMX Centre in Manchester, as they compete for the World Cup.

OLYMPIC TRACK

Even the tracks the pros race on are usually open to the public. The 2012 London Olympic BMX track was one of the most testing courses ever. The men's course was 470 metres long and featured a berm jump, a swooping S-bend and a large table-top jump. The women's track was 430 metres long and, after a series of jumps, headed down through a tunnel. Both courses contained a rhythm section in the final straight.

The course has since been remodelled so it is safe for riders of all levels to use. For example, the starting ramp has been reduced from a whopping eight metres high to just under four metres.

TOP DOG

The only man to win a BMX gold medal at an Olympics is Maris Strombergs from Latvia (below). He won at the Beijing Olympics in 2008 and repeated glory in London in 2012. Strombergs completed the London course in just 37.6 seconds! Nicknamed 'The Machine', Strombergs believes his success is due to starting BMX at the young age of 6.

Rhythm section

Berm jump

Starting ramp

The BMX track used in the 2012 London Olympics is now open to the public.

THE DAY OF THE RACE

BMX race meetings are non-stop, all-day action. Riders have to qualify throughout knockout rounds to reach the final. To come out on top, you need superb bike control, quick reactions and nerves of steel.

RECORD BREAKERS

In 2009 Australian Sam Williams became the only person to win back-to-back Junior World Championships. In 2012 he went on to win the World Cup, become men's World Champion and Olympic silver medallist. He likes racing on tracks that change direction a lot, but still have lots of space to overtake.

MOTOS AND MAINS

There are many classes of BMX race. Riders are put into different races based on age and skill level. Qualifying rounds are called **motos** and contain up to eight riders. In a moto, riders are given points for the place they finish in. At the end of three motos, the riders with the best points qualify for the next round. The final is called the 'main' and decides the overall winner.

Six riders snap out of the starting gate in a qualifying moto.

BATTLING FOR POSITION

Obstacles are not the only thing riders have to worry about. There are up to seven other riders who will do all they can to beat you. You need to be aggressive on the first straight to get into a good position. Riders may use their elbows to force you out of the way – this is part of racing. If you are being squeezed by other riders, the best thing to do is be faster than them. Don't stop pedalling – a pedalling rider is less likely to be knocked down.

OVERTAKING

If you are left behind at the start, don't panic. There is still time to get back in the race. If you stay relaxed, smooth and tidy, you can take advantage of other riders' mistakes and pass them.

You can use any part of the track to overtake. Judge where you think you can pass an opponent. Taking a different line on a berm can be a good move. If you are good at jumping, cornering, or a particular section of track, then that is the best place to overtake. Just stay calm and go for it!

Corners and berms offer up chances to overtake.

17

LIFE OF A PRO: SHANAZE READE

Shanaze Reade has won the BMX World Championships three times and is one of the top cycling stars in the UK. Born in 1988, Reade began racing at the age of 10 when she bought a second-hand BMX bike for £1!

Before discovering BMX Reade had been a keen athlete, competing in 100-metre sprints and the shot put. But then she realised BMX was the best sport to make the most of her strength. Known for her power, Reade developed her strength racing against boys. At the age of 17 she was racing in national races against men and became the second best rider in the UK.

UPS AND DOWNS

BMX racing is an aggressive form of cycling. Injuries and crashes are common. Shanaze Reade is no stranger to the ups and downs of professional racing. Reade has broken bones in her foot, elbow, knee and even her spine, but she has always had the determination to bounce back. In 2006 she won her first Junior World Championships despite earlier injuring her foot. A year later she won her first senior World Championships.

Shanaze Reade on her way to winning her first senior World Championships.

FITNESS AND TRAINING

An important part of being a BMX racer is eating healthily and spending a lot of time training in the gym. In 2007 Reade took up track cycling in the **velodrome** to keep her fit for BMX competition. Amazingly she won a World Championship gold medal with Victoria Pendleton in the team sprint, in only her second track race ever!

AN OLYMPIC DREAM

Reade's dream is still to win a BMX Olympic gold medal. As World Champion, she went into the 2008 Olympics as favourite. But tragedy struck as she crashed out on the final bend while going for victory. In 2009 she could not race because she needed surgery on her shoulder. However the dream was not over. In 2010 she came back and won the World BMX title for the third time.

In 2012 Reade had the chance to win gold at her home Olympics in London. However, she missed out again finishing a disappointing sixth. With her heart still set on Olympic gold in 2016, Reade has now moved out to the USA so she can practise racing against world-class opposition more often.

The Olympic title eluded Reade again in 2012, but she will be back to try for gold in 2016.

FREESTYLE FOR BEGINNERS

If you have bought a BMX to freestyle you probably can't wait to learn lots of amazing tricks. However, it doesn't matter if you are freestyling on the ground, in the air or on obstacles, there are basic tricks everyone needs to learn at the start.

A manual is a simple trick for beginners to perform.

THE MANUAL

The manual is a simple trick for beginners. To do a manual, the rider pops the front wheel up and coasts on the back wheel. It's like a wheelie except you don't pedal.

Start by rolling forwards at a medium speed with the pedals level. Then lean backwards behind the saddle with your arms straight and pull the handlebars towards you. If you pull up too hard you can touch the back brake to bring the wheel back down.

Mastering any trick takes patience. The best way to learn tricks is to practise with another rider. Your friend can be ready to hold the bike if it looks like you are about to fall off.

THE BUNNY HOP

The bunny hop is a crucial building block for many BMX tricks. As you coast forward on the bike, crouch down bending your legs and arms. Lift the handlebars as you stand up straight to get off the ground. To level the bike in mid-air, push back against the pedals and push the handlebars forward. On landing, bend your elbows and knees to absorb the shock.

A rider rises up in the air with their bike to perform a bunny hop.

TOP DOG

Daniel Dhers from Venezuela (right) is one of the most successful BMX freestylers ever. He has won five gold medals at the **X Games** (see pages 28–29). His tip for learning BMX is patience…'When you want to give up, remember that at the end it is always worth it.'

RIDING RAMPS

If you will be riding at skate parks, you need to learn how to ride ramps. Ramps are usually steeper and more slippery than they first look. So you need to get out there and get a feel for the ramps. When you feel confident you can try some simple moves on the ramp like the kick turn. This is when a rider stops with the front wheel in the air at the top of the slope, and then twists the bike around to ride back down.

If you can bunny hop, you can start jumping off ramps. Make sure you have enough speed, and as you roll over the top of the ramp, do a bunny hop to get height on your jump.

REAL CLUB NAUTICO

21

AT THE SKATE PARK

*A skate park is one of the best places to develop your freestyle BMX skills. Skate parks are made of wood or concrete and contain ramps, **bowls** and platforms.*

ON THE HALFPIPE

The most popular type of ramp at the skate park is the halfpipe. Halfpipe ramps look like pipes that have been cut in half. Riders can ride up and down the halfpipe ramps over and over again to gain speed and do tricks. If you plan on becoming a top freestyler you must learn how to pull off **aerial** tricks.

To do a simple aerial, turn the handlebars just before you reach the top of the ramp at speed, and then bunny hop. Use your hips to swing the back wheel around and land facing back down the ramp.

A freestyler performs tricks in a halfpipe.

COPING WITH THE COPING

The tube that runs along the top of the ramp is called the **coping**. Coping is usually made from steel to stop it wearing away. Riders use the coping to perform tricks such as the 'tail tap'. This is when riders bunny hop on to the coping and land on the back wheel. They brake just before they land and hold themselves in position before twisting the bike back down the ramp.

RECORD BREAKERS

Park and street freestyler Garrett Reynolds (right) from the USA has dominated BMX in recent history. At the Barcelona X Games in 2013 Reynolds won the gold medal in the Street event for the sixth time in a row! Later that year in Los Angeles, he had to settle for silver. But Reynolds claimed back his title in 2014 winning his seventh gold medal.

GRINDS

Grinds are stunts where the rider slides part of their bike other than the wheels along a ledge or the coping of a ramp. This is where you can put your axle pegs to good use. Other grinds involve the cranks and pedals.

A 'feeble grind' is the most basic kind of grind. A rider bunny hops and lands the front wheel and a rear axle peg on a ledge. To stop the back peg dropping off as you ride, lean your body towards the ledge slightly.

Holding or sliding both the front and back pegs on a ledge is called a 'double-peg stall' or a 'double-peg grind'. There are all sorts of tricks to learn. Landing the back peg on the coping and balancing it there is called the 'icepick'.

A rider does a double-peg grind on a handrail.

FLATLAND TRICKS

Flatland is the art of performing BMX tricks on nothing but a smooth, flat surface. Riders spin and balance their bike and body into a series of unexpected positions. The pros will spend hours every day perfecting their technique.

Flatland freestylers amaze crowds with their impossible-looking stunts.

In flatland competitions, riders have to link several moves together in a row without stopping. The judges score the riders for their style and flow. Riders also score extra marks for difficult and original tricks. They lose points if a trick is not completed or their foot touches the ground.

THE PUPPET STAND

There are hundreds of flatland tricks so where do you start? The 'puppet stand' is a brilliant trick for a beginner. As well as looking good, it helps a rider get a feel for balancing the bike. Roll the bike forward with the left pedal down and lift your right leg over the frame. Then quickly hop your left foot off and put your right foot on the left pedal. Keep your leg strong and straight. Now you can let go of the handlebars and hold your arms and left leg out to finish the trick.

An endo is one of the more straightforward flatland tricks.

ENDOS AND POGOS

Balancing on the front wheel is called an endo. This is the original flatland trick. Brake the front wheel sharply at low speed and push the handlebars forward to lift the back wheel off the ground. If you do a small endo while standing on the back pegs you can transfer your weight backwards to start pogo jumping on the back wheel.

If you want to get really fancy, you can add some **barspins** while you are pogoing. To barspin, spin the handlebars around with one hand and catch them with your other hand.

TAIL WHIPS

A flatland rider can not only spin the handlebars around – they can spin the whole bike frame around (left). This is called a tail whip. There are many ways to do it. One way is to lift your leg over the frame and jam your foot against the front tyre. Then shift your weight forwards to lift the back wheel up and kick the frame with the other leg so it spins around.

RECORD BREAKERS

Performing a 'cliffhanger spin' means riding the BMX with one foot on the front peg and the other on the handlebars! England's Matti Hemmings took up flatland BMX because he was a fan of **breakdancing**. In 2013, he broke the world record for the number of cliffhanger spins in one minute. His 56 spins, nearly one every second, must have made him dizzy!

25

BIG AIR

A rider flies head over heels on his BMX to perform a back flip.

Vert (short for vertical) riding is the most daring form of BMX event. Riders shoot out of a four-metre-high halfpipe and perform wickedly dangerous stunts high up in the air. Vert is extreme, demanding and takes many years of practice.

SPINS AND FLIPS

On a 360 spin the rider does one full turn before landing back down on the ramp. In mid-air the rider twists their upper body and throws their head back over their shoulders to make the full turn. Once a rider has mastered the 360, they move on to 540, 720 and 900 degree spins! If you want to try big aerial tricks like these you should practise in a **foam pit**. The back flip is the trick that is hard to watch without covering your eyes. As the rider hits the coping they arch their head and body back to go head over heels on the bike.

REMIXES

Adding an extra move to a standard trick or changing a trick slightly is called a remix. Some riders think spins and flips are not mind-blowing enough. They perform tail whips and barspins as they fly, or do the trick no-handed, one-footed or double-pegged. The possibilities are endless.

Dirt jumper and vert rider Anthony Napolitan (below) from the USA has been at the top of the BMX game for years. His special talent is remixing front and back flips. In 2009 he became the first person to land a double, front flip.

SHAPE SHIFTERS

Vert riders can create fantastic shapes high in the air. The 'superman' trick involves the rider taking both feet off the pedals and stretching them out so they look like Superman in flight. On a 'can-can' trick the rider lifts a foot over the other side of the frame and kicks it out sideways.

Many tricks involve the freestyler grabbing part of the bike, such as the front tyre. To do the 'toboggan' stunt, the rider leans back out of the way so that they can grab the nose of the saddle.

DIRT JUMPING

Another high-flying form of freestyle BMX is dirt jumping. Dirt jumpers use huge mounds of dirt to catch big air and do tricks.

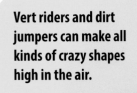

Vert riders and dirt jumpers can make all kinds of crazy shapes high in the air.

THE X GAMES

The X Games is the most important event for BMX freestylers. The Games began in 1995 when it was called the Extreme Games. It has been held every year since and has become the best-known competition for all kinds of extreme sport. Like the Olympics, all the top athletes come together to challenge for a gold medal, and crowds flock to watch the daredevil competitors in action.

STREET AND PARK

At the X Games, the organisers set out an area for the Street competition so it looks like a real part of the town. The course has railings, flower beds and steps. In the Park event, the arena is laid out like a skate park with ramps. In Street, riders focus more on balancing tricks while Park freestylers do more aerial stunts.

Silver medal winner Dennis Enarson grinds up a rail and adds a barspin in the X Games Street event.

THE JUDGES

Riders are usually given three runs to show their skills. In the set time they can use whatever part of the course they want. The judges score the riders for their style, skill and how well they use the time and the obstacles. Difficult and original tricks are given big scores. Showmanship, the ability to present your routine to the crowd, is also important.

Morgan Wade of the USA makes a giant leap in the Big Air competition at the 2012 X Games.

ESPN3.com

X GAMES

VERT AND DIRT

There are also gold medals to be won in Vert and Dirt Jumping at the X Games. The craziest event is the Big Air competition. Riders bomb down a ramp ten storeys high and pull an impossible stunt while jumping over an 18-metre wide gap, before landing into a halfpipe the other side. The riders take turns to perform their terrifying stunts. Big Air is always punishing on the athletes. Riders frequently crash down hard on the ramps – it's all part of the job!

TOP DOG

Britain's Jamie Bestwick (left) is in a class of his own in the BMX Vert competition. After winning the Vert silver medal in 2006 he has since won the gold medal at every single X Games. His eight victories in a row set a record for any extreme sport at the X Games. His trademark moves are backflips with twists (called flairs) at huge heights. Bestwick never imagined he would become a BMX legend. He started riding BMX at the age of 10 as a way to hang out with friends. At 13 he started entering local events just for fun but has gradually become unbeatable.

FIND OUT MORE

BOOKS

BMX (Adrenalin Rush),
Aj Anderson, (Franklin Watts 2011)

BMX Bicycle Racing: Techniques and Tricks,
Brian Wingate, (Rosen 2003)

Freestyle BMX (Radar),
Isobel Thomas, (Wayland 2013)

Freestyle BMX Tricks: Flatland and Air,
Sean D'Arcy, (A & C Black 2010)

WEBSITES

http://www.wikihow.com/Category:BMX
A series of 'How to…' guides for BMX owners

www.uci.ch/templates/UCI/UCI8/layout.asp?MenuId=MTY3NDk&LangId=1
The website for the UCI, cycling's governing body, contains the latest news, results and rider rankings

http://bmxtraining.com
Articles to help BMX racers train and ride better

www.britishcycling.org.uk/bmx/article/20131213-Get-into-BMX-0#Race
Find a BMX club or race near you

www.wrekinriders.co.uk/How-To.php
Tips on starting out, buying a bike and racing

www.bmxtricksnow.com
A guide to the most popular freestyle tricks

www.bmxinsight.com
Articles on bikes and gear for BMX freestylers

Website disclaimer: Note to parents and teachers: Every effort has been made by the Publishers to ensure that these websites are suitable for children, that they are of the highest educational value, and that they contain no inappropriate or offensive material. However, because of the nature of the Internet, it is impossible to guarantee that the contents of these sites will not be altered. We strongly advise that Internet access is supervised by a responsible adult.

GLOSSARY

aerial BMX tricks performed high in the air, such as spins and flips

barspin spin the handlebars 360 degrees while letting go of them

berm a banked corner made entirely of dirt or covered in tarmac or concrete

bowl a concrete or wooden area of a skate park shaped like a breakfast bowl

breakdancing fast and acrobatic dancing where different parts of the body are used to touch the ground

coping the protective metal edge running along the top of a ramp

downslope the downward slope of a hill

foam pit a soft landing area designed with a bed of foam blocks, used by riders to reduce the risk of injury when they are practising extreme stunts

halfpipe a U-shaped ramp, which riders can ride up and down to perform a variety of tricks

moto a BMX race in which riders attempt to place high enough in order to qualify for the final

pegs the four tube-shaped platforms attached to the bike's wheels, which freestylers can use to place their feet on during stunts

sponsor an organisation that helps a rider with the cost of gear and travel in return for some form of advertising

starting gate a barrier that is raised at the start of a BMX race

velodrome a sports arena with a banked, oval track for bike racing

vert a large ramp where the walls become vertical towards the top

visor a screen that can be pulled down to cover the face to protect the rider's eyes from the sun and flying objects

X Games a sports event where competitors compete for gold, silver and bronze medals in a variety of extreme sports

INDEX